The Life of
Alvin Ailey

by Tim McLean

Orlando   Boston   Dallas   Chicago   San Diego

Visit *The Learning Site!*
www.harcourtschool.com

An American Artist

Alvin Ailey was one of America's most unique and most celebrated artists. During his lifetime, Ailey created seventy-nine ballets, and throughout his career, numerous dance and choreography awards were bestowed upon him. He also founded the Alvin Ailey American Dance Theater company, and to this day, the beauty of his many works continues to reach wide-ranging audiences. Perhaps Alvin Ailey's greatest and most revolutionary contribution, however, was his special vision of dance: He sought to infuse a sense of social awareness within the art form of dance. All these achievements came from a man who began life as an impoverished child born in rural Texas—more than a thousand miles away from the lights of Broadway that would one day blaze out his name.

The Early Years

Alvin Ailey was born on January 5, 1931, in Rogers, Texas. He was raised by his mother, Lula Elizabeth Cliff. Alvin and his mother were very poor. They moved around Texas in those early years, at times picking cotton for a living. The two had only each other to depend on through many hard times. As a result, they developed a close bond. One of the larger towns in Texas that Alvin and his mother eventually moved to was Navasota. It was also a segregated community, with the African-American population largely isolated in one section of the city. It was here that Ailey first encountered the work of African-American actors, singers, and dancers.

He attended theaters and blues clubs, which opened his eyes to the excitement of the performing arts. Before this, Ailey's only experience with African-American performances had come as a result of attending church regularly with his mother. There he witnessed the beauty of melodious Baptist gospel music.

When Ailey turned twelve, he and his mother moved to Los Angeles, California. The two continued to live in poverty, often not having enough to eat, but together they persevered. In school, young Alvin spent much of his time drawing and painting, and he also had a gift for languages. Some of his teachers recognized his talent and expected him to become a painter or poet, if he were to choose a career in the arts. As yet, however, young Alvin Ailey had not discovered the art form that would allow him to express his creativity.

3

Young Ailey Discovers Dance

While living in Los Angeles, Alvin Ailey attended several performances that would shape the rest of his life. It was the first of these performances that helped him choose the path his art would take. This revelation occurred on a junior high school field trip during which Ailey, at thirteen years of age, was taken to see a presentation of the Ballet Russe de Monte Carlo, a Russian-style ballet company.

More About Ballet

Ballet is a tradition of dance that originated in Europe in the mid-1600s. Ballet had its greatest popularity in France, which is why so many ballet terms come from the French language. Russian-style ballet is known for its leaps and exciting maneuvers in the air. It was this ballet style that first captured the imagination of the young Alvin Ailey, an influence that found its way into his unique choreography.

Ailey was in awe of the show. The flawless movements, the dancers flying through the air, the music, the precision—everything worked together to mesmerize the young teen. Later, in his autobiography, he would claim that at that very moment he knew he wanted to be involved in dance for the rest of his life.

Dance was suddenly all Alvin Ailey could talk about, and he began spending every free moment in downtown Los Angeles, which in the 1940s had a thriving theater district. He watched the performances of Janet Collins, one of the only famous African-American ballerinas during the forties. Ailey also admired Katherine Dunham, perhaps the most influential African-American dancer of her time. Ailey would visit this vibrant performer in her dressing room whenever she was in town for a show. Dunham became one of the young man's role models, and he would later pay tribute to her life and to her work in his own life and art.

5

Ailey watched these performances and was urged repeatedly by friends to pursue his interest in dance. The best-known dance instructor in the area at the time was Lester Horton, who ran America's first racially integrated dance studio. Ailey stalled for six months, afraid of being rejected. Finally, a change in his personal life propelled him forward: Ailey's mother had decided to remarry.

More About Katherine Dunham

Katherine Dunham earned her doctoral degree in anthropology and spent long periods of her life conducting studies in the Caribbean, the West Indies, and Africa. She also started her own all-black dance troupe, choreographed dances for Broadway and motion pictures, opened the Dunham School of Dance in New York, became the first African-American choreographer at the Metropolitan Opera in New York, authored several books, and started cultural arts programs for disadvantaged youths in Illinois. Her unique dance style, as well as her drive to make dance and other cultural arts a part of the African-American experience had a profound effect on the goals Alvin Ailey set for his career.

> **More About Modern Dance**
>
> Modern dance first arose as a rebellion against the conventions of ballet; thus it is usually defined by how it is different from the ballet tradition. Whereas ballet uses a set of prescribed motions and steps, modern dancers are free to create their own steps and types of movements. Their movements can be freer, since they do not need to face the audience or retain an upright posture, as dancers do in ballet. Modern dance also does not require the dancers' movements to parallel the rhythms of the music. In fact, sometimes music is not necessary at all. Modern dance brings to the stage a creative and expressive language for dancers to use in conveying their emotions to the audience. This expressiveness would serve to enhance the social commentary on African-American history in Alvin Ailey's choreography.

Her life would be changing. Alvin Ailey realized that he needed to move ahead with his own life. With mixed emotions, he decided to interview with Mr. Horton.

Ailey was accepted into the Horton studio and began training immediately. The routine was difficult, and Ailey devoted virtually all his time to the art and craft of dance. Lester Horton taught classical ballet, but he also emphasized modern-dance techniques. This emphasis helped shape Ailey's rigorous yet expressive style of dance. The young man studied under Horton for years, and in many ways, the Horton studio became Ailey's second home and family.

Ailey's Career Begins

In 1953, Lester Horton passed away. Alvin Ailey, only twenty-three years old and barely finished with his apprenticeship period, was named as Horton's replacement. Suddenly, he would be responsible for the company as its new artistic director. Ailey grieved terribly for his friend and teacher, but he was through wasting time. He put all his energy into the company as a way to honor Horton's memory. Ailey choreographed several ballets in the next year and a half, and his reputation as a major talent grew quickly.

When opportunity next presented itself, Ailey grabbed it without hesitation. While on tour in 1954, he was offered a role in a Broadway musical, *House of Flowers,* and he took it. From then on, Ailey made his home in New York City, one of the centers of the arts in America.

Ailey took advantage of all that New York had to offer. He attended lectures, dramas, operas, musicals, and poetry readings. He studied in every library he could find and met with any career artist who would see him. While in New York, he studied with many

important dancers, including Martha Graham, who is one of the most influential choreographers in the history of modern dance.

House of Flowers was a Broadway success, and it enabled Ailey to begin working with some very famous people. He actually ended up choreographing with Katherine Dunham, the same woman he had revered as a child.

More About Martha Graham

Martha Graham studied dance at the prestigious Denishawn school. When she started dancing and directing on her own, Graham moved away from the elaborate style she had studied and invented a style of her own that made her famous. Her costumes and staging were simple, yet her movements were severe and sharp. In training other dancers, Graham focused on angular body movements, contraction and release of body parts, and contact with the ground. Her style was well known for being emotional and expressive. Graham's innovations influenced Ailey as a dancer and choreographer by introducing him to movements that were thought of as revolutionary at the time.

More About the Civil Rights Movement

The incident that came to be known as the Montgomery Bus Boycott played a pivotal part in the Civil Rights movement. In 1955, an African-American woman named Rosa Parks refused to give up her seat to a white man while on a segregated bus in Montgomery, Alabama. Parks was arrested. One of the leaders of the Civil Rights movement, the Reverend Dr. Martin Luther King Jr. worked to put Parks's arrest into the national spotlight. King mobilized African Americans to protest the arrest of Rosa Parks, urging them to participate in a bus boycott. The highly successful boycott lasted more than a year. King went on to become the most famous spokesman of the movement. The social and political activism of the movement deeply affected Alvin Ailey and became the backdrop against which he set many of his most famous works.

Ailey's Work Finds Focus

Alvin Ailey began to get regular jobs dancing for television shows and movies. He choreographed and had leading roles in Broadway musicals, and his reputation as a talented artist continued to grow. Ailey felt happy and fulfilled as a part of this prominent theatrical scene. Soon, however, his work would take a new and more important turn. The time was the late 1950s, and the American Civil Rights movement was under way. African-American men and women all over the country were demanding equal rights and calling for an end to the hatred and discrimination that had come to define much of American social history.

At this point in his life, Ailey chose to take his art to an even higher level. The social upheaval of the Civil Rights movement and black history in America became his focus. He wanted to communicate with his art, and the struggles of African Americans became a central subject for him for the rest of his career. He began to envision dances that portrayed the stories of black men and women throughout history and that showcased the beauty and grace of African-American dancers. Ailey had a message to deliver, one promoting the idea of equality among the races of the world. He knew he could spread his message through his art. Similar to making speeches or writing, dance was a way to reach large numbers of people.

Alvin Ailey's biographer, Jennifer Dunning, said that for Ailey, dance was "a way to communicate with whoever turned up to see his work, whether he was speaking about the power of the blues in black lives, [or] the beauty of those lives."

In 1960, Alvin Ailey choreographed what is considered to be his masterpiece, the work called "Revelations." This spectacle combines many African, classical, and modern dances with beautiful imagery. The music is a mix of lilting gospel numbers, African folk songs, and classical orchestra pieces. "Revelations" celebrates the faith of humankind. The work also depicts the struggles of African Americans throughout history. From the instant that the first strains of music began, the work was a critical and commercial success, making the Alvin Ailey dance company famous. Today, more than forty years later, "Revelations" is still performed by the Ailey dancers, bringing joy to new generations of people.

Ailey toured with his company, the Alvin Ailey American Dance Theater, and performed in places such as Africa, France, and Russia. As the years passed, he danced less and less and

More About Judith Jamison

Judith Jamison studied at the Philadelphia Dance Academy. Her height (almost six feet), strength, and elegance made her stand out immediately, and she made her debut with the American Ballet Theatre in the early 1960s. She was recruited by Alvin Ailey in 1965 and soon became one of the stars of the troupe. Ailey created a famous solo role for Jamison in "Cry," a celebration of African-American women. Jamison started her own company, The Jamison Project, in 1988, but upon Ailey's death in 1989, she became the director of the Ailey dance company and merged her company into his. Jamison's imposing interpretations of Ailey's works enhanced the Ailey dance tradition.

spent more time writing and choreographing, as well as managing his large network of dance schools. New stars joined the company, such as the great Judith Jamison, who years later would take Ailey's place as director. Alvin Ailey won numerous dance awards given in the United States, but perhaps his greatest achievement was not a particular dance or show. Instead, Ailey's greatest legacy was his creative spirit and commitment to the arts as a means of spreading social awareness.

Inspiring A New Generation

In 1984, Alvin Ailey started a new project. He began researching the life of jazz saxophonist Charlie Parker in preparation for a work depicting his life. Ailey spent time in Kansas City, Missouri, a center of jazz where Parker had spent many years. There Ailey encountered many poor, disadvantaged children. Their plight reminded him of his own difficult youth. In response, he set up the first AileyCamp in Kansas City, Missouri, and today there are others in Chicago, New York, Boston, and Bridgeport, Connecticut, with more planned each year. AileyCamps recruit young people between the ages of 11 and 14 and introduce them to dance and to the arts. These camps, however, are much more than dance schools. They concentrate on personal development as well as on education. Ailey realized how important exposure to an artistic "spark" can be to young people in helping them to gain the confidence they need to achieve their dreams.

Final Years

Alvin Ailey's health declined through the late eighties, but not before he was invited to the White House to meet with the President. Ailey later wrote that he considered this one of the greatest honors of his life. In 1988, he received a Kennedy Center Honors award for his lifetime contribution to American culture through the performing arts. Alvin Ailey died in a New York hospital on December 1, 1989, after a long illness. His passing was mourned by the hundreds of dancers he had taught and had worked with, and by legions of fans in America and overseas who had been affected by his work. At his memorial service the acclaimed American poet Maya Angelou compared his death with the falling of a great tree.

More than a decade has passed since this unique and talented artist died, but his influence continues. Alvin Ailey brought the themes of the Civil Rights movement directly into the world of performing arts, creating dance works that cry out for the equality of all and for the appreciation of diversity.

Even more impressive is what Ailey did for dance itself. Dance had formerly been taught in small groups, and because such lessons were costly, they were usually accessible only to the privileged. Ailey realized how unlikely his own entrance into the dance world had been, and he was determined to open the doors to more young people. For more than fifteen years, AileyCamps have been welcoming underprivileged young people to a world that at one time was off-limits to them. Many AileyCamp graduates go on to become wonderful dancers, but the real drive behind the program is to empower them to become whatever they want to be.

This contribution, plus the vision to use dance as a means of inspiring social consciousness, make Alvin Ailey one of America's greatest artists and citizens.

THE LIFE OF ALVIN AILEY

1931	born on January 5, in Rogers, Texas
1942	moved to Los Angeles, California; first became aware of dance as an art form
1953	named artistic director of the Lester Horton Dance Theater
1954	moved to New York City; performed on Broadway in *House of Flowers*
1958	founded the Alvin Ailey American Dance Theater
1960	choreographed "Revelations"
1970	toured Russia to high acclaim
1984	visited Kansas City, Missouri; began the first AileyCamp there
1988	received the Kennedy Center Honors award
1989	died on December 1, in New York